GEOGRAPHY QUEST

MOUNTAIN PEAK PERIL

JOHN TOWNSEND

QED Publishing

Cover Design: Punch Bowl Design
Illustrator: David Shephard
Editor: Claudia Martin
Designer: Carol Davis
QED Project Editors: Ruth Symons and
Carly Madden
QED Project Designer: Rachel Lawston
Editorial Director: Victoria Garrard
Art Director: Laura Roberts-Jensen

Copyright © QED Publishing 2015

First published in the UK in 2015 by
QED Publishing, A Quarto Group company,
The Old Brewery, 6 Blundell Street,
London, N7 9BH

www.qed-publishing.co.uk

A catalogue record for this book is available
from the British Library.

ISBN 978 1 78493 029 5

Printed in China

Picture credits: Shutterstock: bioraven 5-43;
ekler 5-43; Evlakhov Valeriy 10; Monti26 5-43;
narcisse 10; Palsu 5-43; Patrick Poendl 37.

How to begin
your adventure

Are you ready for an amazing adventure that will test your brain power to the limit – full of mind-bending puzzles, twists and turns? Then you've come to the right place!

Mountain Peak Peril is no ordinary book – you don't read the pages in order, 1, 2, 3...

Instead you jump forwards and backwards through the book as you face a series of challenges. Sometimes you may lose your way, but the story will always guide you back to where you need to be.

The story begins on page 4. Straight away, there are questions to answer and problems to overcome. The questions will look something like this:

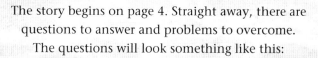

IF YOU THINK THE CORRECT ANSWER IS A, GO TO PAGE 10 **A**

IF YOU THINK THE CORRECT ANSWER IS B, GO TO PAGE 18 **B**

Your task is to solve each problem. If you think the correct answer is A, turn to page 10 and look for the same symbol in red. That's where you will find the next part of the story. If you make the wrong choice, the text will explain where you went wrong and let you have another go.

The problems in this adventure are about mountains and their features. To solve them, you must use your geography skills. To help you, there's a glossary of useful words at the back of the book, starting on page 44.

ARE YOU READY?
Turn the page and let your adventure begin!

MOUNTAIN PEAK PERIL

You've been called urgently to Television Wildlife Centre.
Lucinda Lavender, the TV Director General, is waiting for you.

We desperately need your help.
We've heard reports of a terrifying
yeti in the Towering Mountains. We sent
a film crew and our top wildlife presenter,
Sir Digby Tweedhope, over there to film it —
but they disappeared without trace a week
ago. With your amazing geography skills,
you'll be able to find them.

Get your snow boots and climbing gear.
This is a life or death mission.

COMING SOON ...
SIR DIGBY
AND THE YETI

RUSH TO PAGE 14
**TO SET OFF ON YOUR
MOUNTAIN ADVENTURE**

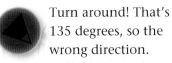

Turn around! That's 135 degrees, so the wrong direction.

GO BACK TO PAGE 38 AND TRY AGAIN

That's not right.

GO BACK TO PAGE 36 AND TRY AGAIN

Correct. Aspect is the direction to which a mountain slope faces.

You trudge to the right spot. There are no footprints in the empty snow. You check Sir Digby's last blog entry:

"I can feel the ground moving – and look at all that snow. Oh no! It's an a…"

That's strange: you can feel the ground moving too!

Think fast! What was Sir Digby going to say?

IT'S AN ATTACK BY THE YETI.
GO TO PAGE 23

IT'S AN ACTIVE VOLCANO.
HEAD TO PAGE 19

IT'S AN AVALANCHE.
TURN TO PAGE 27

Luckily, that was the right rope. You climb to the top of the cliff, where you have a dizzying view of the mountain summit.

You have reached the snowline: the ground up here is covered in snow and you can't see any more cairns. You check Sir Digby's blog and read the next entry:

"I hiked all the way along the ribbon lake,
then climbed up through the corrie,
with an arête on my right."

*Which of the three
routes to the summit
did Sir Digby take?*

A.
GO TO PAGE 23

A. GO TO PAGE 23

B.
TURN TO PAGE 17

B. TURN TO PAGE 17

C.
FLIP TO PAGE 20

C. FLIP TO PAGE 20

That's not right.

**TURN BACK
TO PAGE 42
AND TRY AGAIN**

Wrong way!
That's 90 degrees.

**TURN BACK TO PAGE 38
AND THINK AGAIN**

That's right. A cairn is a pile of stones left as a marker. Scree means the small, loose rocks lying on a mountain slope.

You climb past another of Sir Digby's cairns and see a cliff rising in front of you. Three ropes are dangling down it.

There's a note:

> Two of these ropes aren't tied to anything. Answer this question to choose the right rope and climb safely up the cliff. Many mountains were formed when the plates in the Earth's crust moved towards each other and made the crust crumple.
>
> What are such mountains called?

IF YOU THINK IT'S VOLCANIC MOUNTAINS, GRAB THE GREEN ROPE.

GO TO PAGE 10

IF YOU THINK IT'S BLOCK MOUNTAINS, GRAB THE BLUE ROPE.

TURN TO PAGE 12

IF YOU THINK IT'S FOLD MOUNTAINS, GRAB THE RED ROPE.

HEAD TO PAGE 7

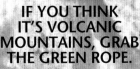

"That is the truth." Mountains are the 'water towers' of the world. They supply between 60% and 80% of the Earth's fresh water, because all major rivers begin in the mountains.

The monk opens a door and pushes you roughly inside. What's going on?

TURN TO PAGE 29
TO FIND OUT

That's far too high.

TURN BACK TO PAGE 39
TO TRY AGAIN FAST

Wrong answer.

TURN BACK TO PAGE 37
AND TRY AGAIN

No, commercial farming is when crops and animals are produced to sell for a profit. Most farming in the mountains is subsistence farming, when crops and animals are produced to feed just the farmer's family.

TURN BACK TO PAGE 16
AND TRY AGAIN

No, volcanic mountains are formed by volcanoes, when molten rock inside the Earth erupts and piles up at the surface.

TURN BACK TO PAGE 8 AND GRAB ANOTHER ROPE QUICKLY

Wrong direction. Hydroelectric power (building dams and using water power to drive turbines to make electricity) is important in many mountain areas.

TURN BACK TO PAGE 35 AND THINK AGAIN

1/10

Correct. The leeward side is on the opposite side of the mountain from the one on which the wind usually blows (windward side).

The wind is blowing strongly here, so you continue round the mountain until you can't feel any gusts. The altimeter reads 2100 metres. You spot a padlocked metal box.

To open me, you'll need the right number combination. In what year did Edmund Hillary and Tenzing Norgay become the first people to climb Mount Everest?

1492.
GO TO
PAGE 16

1492

1666.
GO TO
PAGE 37

1666

1953.
HEAD TO
PAGE 40

1953

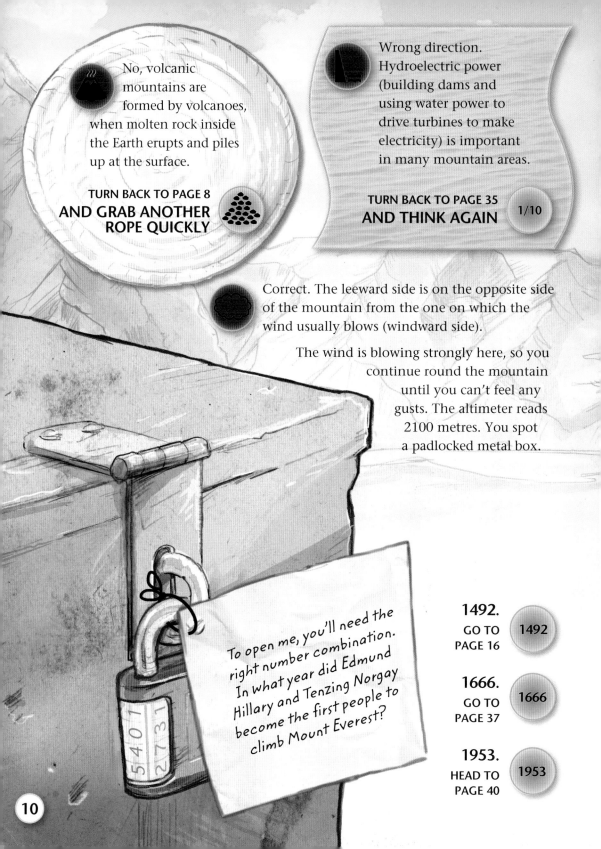

As your eyes adjust to the gloom, you realize you are in a cavern.

Hello, I'm Dorothy, camerawoman for Sir Digby Tweedhope. This is Geoff, our director. We stopped here to rest, but Sir Digby didn't want to lose the yeti's trail, so he went on alone.

Two paths lead up the mountain from here. Digby texted us a clue about which path he took so we could follow him. But we can't solve it.

Geoff hands you his phone.

Where is the world's longest mountain range?

Take the left path if it's South America. Take the right path if it's under the sea.

Which path should you take?

SOUTH AMERICA = LEFT. ◀

GO TO PAGE 39

UNDER THE SEA = RIGHT. ▶

GO TO PAGE 36

Correct. Northeast is 45 degrees from north. Degrees are always measured clockwise – the same direction a clock's hands move. You're off on the right track and heading northeast up a winding mountain path.

After hiking for a while, you check your altimeter: you're nearly at 2000 metres above sea level. The next entry on Sir Digby's blog reads:

"We came across some extraordinary evidence!
We hid it for safe-keeping on the leeward mountain slope at 2100 metres."

*Where will you find
the evidence?*

**ON THE STEEPEST SIDE
OF THE MOUNTAIN.**
TURN TO PAGE 17

**ON THE SIDE SHELTERED
FROM THE WIND.**
GO TO PAGE 10

**ON THE SLOPE
FACING THE SUN.**
HEAD TO PAGE 18

*"You have
chosen wrongly."*

**TURN BACK
TO PAGE 21
AND CHOOSE
AGAIN**

No, block mountains are formed when faults, or cracks, in the Earth's crust force some blocks of rock up and others down.

**GO BACK TO PAGE 8
AND GRAB
ANOTHER ROPE**

 No, Sir Digby wouldn't have seen grass above the snowline. That's the line on a mountain above which there is always snow and ice.

GO BACK TO PAGE 20 AND THINK AGAIN

 The building looks like a temple. Your path to it is blocked by a gate. A notice reads:

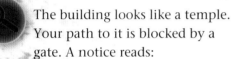

ONLY MOUNTAIN PILGRIMS WELCOME. PASSWORD REQUIRED (TO MAKE SURE THE YETI CAN'T ENTER). WHICH IS THE HIGHEST MOUNTAIN FROM BASE TO PEAK?

 MOUNT EVEREST.
GO TO PAGE 43

 MAUNA KEA.
HEAD TO PAGE 32

K2.
TURN TO PAGE 37

 Incorrect.

GO BACK TO PAGE 42 AND THINK AGAIN

You arrive at a base camp in the foothills of the Towering Mountains. This is where Sir Digby set off on his search for the yeti.

A grumpy mountain rescue officer greets you.

Thinking of heading up there?
We won't let you be a risk to people who live and work in the mountains. You must answer some questions to show you understand this environment.

Our altitude here is 1500 metres.
But what does altitude mean?

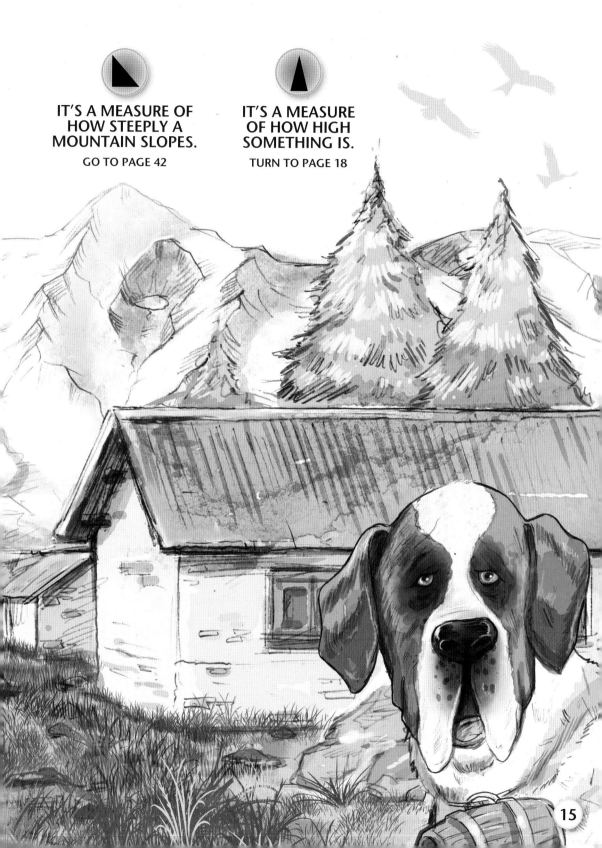

IT'S A MEASURE OF
HOW STEEPLY A
MOUNTAIN SLOPES.

GO TO PAGE 42

IT'S A MEASURE
OF HOW HIGH
SOMETHING IS.

TURN TO PAGE 18

15

No, that was the year that Christopher Columbus landed in America.

TURN BACK TO PAGE 10 AND TRY AGAIN

No, that's an ice cap.

GO BACK TO PAGE 37 AND HAVE ANOTHER TRY

That's right. Many mountain farmers take their animals to lower pastures for winter.

You and the goats head down towards a ramshackle farmhouse. The farmer reappears and cooks you a delicious stew.

It will be dark soon. If you can answer this question, I'll let you sleep by the fire.

How do mountain farmers grow crops up here on steep slopes with thin soil?

TERRACE FARMING.
GO TO PAGE 19

COMMERCIAL FARMING.
TURN TO PAGE 9

INTENSIVE FARMING.
HEAD TO PAGE 21

That's the wrong way. You should have walked all the way along the ribbon lake rather than turning right and climbing up through the hanging valley.

GO BACK TO PAGE 7
AND START AGAIN

That's too high.

TURN BACK TO PAGE 39
**TO TRY AGAIN
BEFORE BANDIT
BILL GETS BACK**

Don't go in that door, whatever you do!

GO BACK TO PAGE 32
AND TRY AGAIN

No, the steepest side may not be the leeward side of the mountain.

TURN BACK TO PAGE 12
AND THINK AGAIN

 Wrong door. Close it quickly!

TURN BACK TO PAGE 32 AND TRY AGAIN

 No, the sun-facing slope may not be the leeward side of the mountain.

GO BACK TO PAGE 12 AND THINK AGAIN

Yes, altitude means height above sea level. Mountains have an altitude of at least 600 metres.

That's not right. There's no snow this far down the mountain.

TURN BACK TO PAGE 36 AND TRY AGAIN

Not bad, but now answer this to prove you really know your stuff:

Which of these happens as altitude increases?

PEOPLE MOVE MORE SLOWLY.
HEAD TO PAGE 20

THERE IS A GREATER RISK OF EARTHQUAKES.
GO TO PAGE 26

IT GETS COLDER.
TURN TO PAGE 30

That's right. The sides of the mountain are cut into wide steps, called terraces. These help to stop the soil from washing away when it rains.

You spend a cosy night in front of the fire. In the morning, the farmer wakes you with a bowl of porridge.

I had some other overnight guests just last week.

"Was it Sir Digby?" you ask.

I'll tell you about them if you can answer this question: How many people in the world live in mountain areas?

Wrong choice. There's no sign of ash, lava or smoke here, so you can't be on an active volcano.

GO BACK TO PAGE 5
AND THINK AGAIN

1 IN EVERY 10 PEOPLE. 1/10
GO TO PAGE 34

1 IN EVERY 100 PEOPLE. 1/100
HEAD TO PAGE 23

1 IN EVERY 1000 PEOPLE. 1/1000
FLICK TO PAGE 27

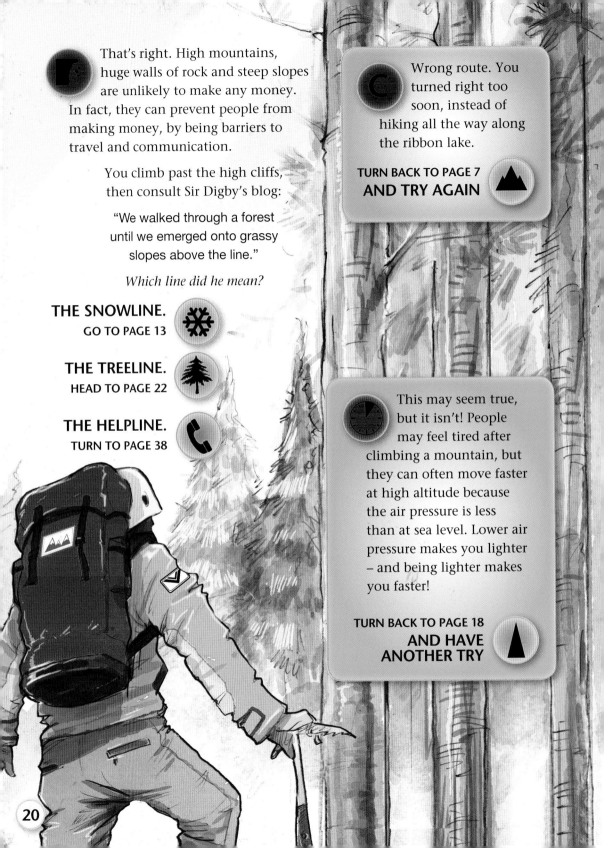

That's right. High mountains, huge walls of rock and steep slopes are unlikely to make any money. In fact, they can prevent people from making money, by being barriers to travel and communication.

You climb past the high cliffs, then consult Sir Digby's blog:

"We walked through a forest until we emerged onto grassy slopes above the line."

Which line did he mean?

THE SNOWLINE.
GO TO PAGE 13

THE TREELINE.
HEAD TO PAGE 22

THE HELPLINE.
TURN TO PAGE 38

Wrong route. You turned right too soon, instead of hiking all the way along the ribbon lake.

TURN BACK TO PAGE 7 AND TRY AGAIN

This may seem true, but it isn't! People may feel tired after climbing a mountain, but they can often move faster at high altitude because the air pressure is less than at sea level. Lower air pressure makes you lighter – and being lighter makes you faster!

TURN BACK TO PAGE 18 AND HAVE ANOTHER TRY

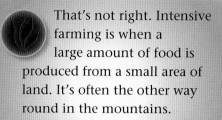

That's not right. Intensive farming is when a large amount of food is produced from a small area of land. It's often the other way round in the mountains.

GO BACK TO PAGE 16 AND THINK AGAIN

 "PASSWORD INCORRECT." A dollop is not a geographical term.

TURN BACK TO PAGE 28 AND TRY AGAIN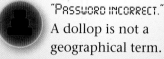

 Correct. The door creaks open and you are faced by a monk,

Have you come to find the truth?

"I've come to find Sir Digby," you say.

You shall find him, if you can tell me the truth about mountains. Without them, much of our planet would die. Is that the truth?

YES. GO TO PAGE 9 ✔

NO. TURN TO PAGE 12 ✗

Correct. Trees can grow only where there is enough warmth and soil. The treeline is the height up a mountain where trees stop growing, often between 2000 and 3000 metres.

You scramble along a ledge above a cliff. Suddenly the ledge gives way – and you are hanging by your fingertips! A face appears.

I'll save you if you're not that terrible Bandit Bill I've heard about. He kidnaps lone travellers in these mountains.

I'm a geographer, not a bandit!

Prove it! Which is the highest mountain in Europe?

MOUNT MCKINLEY.
GO TO PAGE 28

KILIMANJARO.
TURN TO PAGE 31

MOUNT ELBRUS.
HEAD TO PAGE 26

A

You've chosen the correct route. A ribbon lake is a long, narrow lake. A corrie is a bowl-shaped hollow at the top of a mountain valley. An arête is a rugged mountain ridge.

A blizzard blows up but there's no shelter.
You battle on, frozen and exhausted.
At last, you spot buildings.

You hammer on an icy door.

A woman peers out through a hatch.

Help, let me in! I'm a geographer!

You can come in if you give me the password. It's the answer to this question: Where is the highest capital city in the world?

THE ENTOTO MOUNTAINS.
GO TO PAGE 26

THE HIMALAYAS.
GO TO PAGE 28

THE PYRENEES MOUNTAINS.
TURN TO PAGE 30

THE ANDES MOUNTAINS.
FLICK TO PAGE 33

Wrong answer.

TURN BACK TO PAGE 19
AND GUESS AGAIN

No. You can't see any footprints, so that can't be what's happening to you.

TURN BACK TO PAGE 5
AND TRY AGAIN

You and Sir Digby
abseil down the rope.
You reach solid ground
just as Bandit Bill
slashes the rope!

But what's that hairy creature? Could it be... surely not... the yeti?

No, altitude has nothing to do with earthquakes.

GO BACK TO PAGE 18 AND THINK AGAIN

No, the highest capital in Africa is Addis Ababa (capital of Ethiopia) in the Entoto Mountains – but at only 2355 metres it's not the highest capital city in the world.

TURN BACK TO PAGE 23 AND TRY AGAIN A

That's right. At 5642 metres, Mount Elbrus in Russia is the highest mountain in Europe.

Your rescuer hauls you to safety.

My gold mine isn't far from here. I'll take you there if you like. You might like to meet my other visitors!

Could it be Sir Digby and his team? The gold miner leads you into a cave.

It's dark, cold and deathly silent. Is it a trap?

TURN TO PAGE 11 TO FIND OUT WHAT – OR WHO – IS HIDING INSIDE THE MINE

That's right. Avalanches happen when slabs of snow break loose from a mountainside and sweep downhill at speeds of up to 130 kilometres per hour.

You run behind a boulder. You're just in time: a speeding wall of snow rushes past, snatching away your right glove and phone.

Could Sir Digby have been buried by an avalanche? You hear voices and follow the sound until you reach a great field of ice. A sign says:

"STAY OFF ICE.
GLACIOLOGISTS ONLY."

Is it safe to cross the ice?

NO, IT'S AN ARMY FIRING RANGE.
HEAD TO PAGE 31

YES, IT'S A GLACIER.
TURN TO PAGE 37

Incorrect.

GO BACK TO PAGE 19
AND TRY AGAIN

"PASSWORD INCORRECT." Terrain means a stretch of land.

TURN BACK TO PAGE 28
AND TRY AGAIN

No, Mount McKinley (6194 metres) is the highest mountain in North America.

TURN BACK TO PAGE 22 AND TRY AGAIN

Nope. The highest capital city in the Himalayas is Thimphu, capital of Bhutan. At 2648 metres, it's the world's third highest capital.

TURN BACK TO PAGE 23 AND THINK AGAIN

A

Correct choice: that was the false statement. The front of a glacier is called its snout. The glaciologist gives you a glove. You ask if he has seen Sir Digby.

"I haven't, but you can check the webcam. The computer's in that tent."

ENTER PASSWORD

Clue: Name the mounds of rock left behind when a glacier melts.

What's the password?

MORAINE.
GO TO PAGE 31

TERRAIN.
HEAD TO PAGE 27

DOLLOPS.
TURN TO PAGE 21

You've found Sir Digby – at last! But he's clearly being held prisoner here. And that's no monk – it's a mountain bandit!

"I'm Bandit Bill — and that's the truth for you!" guffaws the bandit, slamming the door shut on you.

Please untie me! Bandit Bill is holding me prisoner until the TV station pays him a ransom. The only escape is through that locked door.

You examine the number keypad on the door's lock.

Bill says he wants the ransom money to buy a ski chalet on the 'white mountain' in France. Could that be a clue?

Which French mountain could be the 'white mountain'?

BEN NEVIS.
GO TO PAGE 33

MONT BLANC.
TURN TO PAGE 39

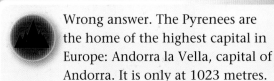

Wrong answer. The Pyrenees are the home of the highest capital in Europe: Andorra la Vella, capital of Andorra. It is only at 1023 metres.

TURN BACK TO PAGE 23 AND TRY AGAIN

That's right. On average, temperature drops by 0.65°C every 100 metres you climb. A mountain summit at 3000 metres could be up to 30°C colder than at its base at sea level.

Before he will let you go, the officer demands to look through your backpack. He pulls out three items.

There's no point carrying extra baggage. You can leave one of these items behind.

Which item do you not need in the mountains?

SUN CREAM. FLICK TO PAGE 33

MALARIA TABLETS. GO TO PAGE 38

THICK GLOVES. TURN TO PAGE 36

No, at 5895 metres Kilimanjaro is the highest mountain in Africa.

GO BACK TO PAGE 22 AND TRY AGAIN

That's the wrong answer. Glaciologists have nothing to do with weapons.

TURN BACK TO PAGE 27 AND TRY AGAIN

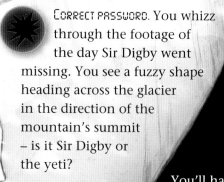

Correct password. You whizz through the footage of the day Sir Digby went missing. You see a fuzzy shape heading across the glacier in the direction of the mountain's summit – is it Sir Digby or the yeti?

You'll have to head for the summit yourself to find out. The thin air makes it harder and harder to breathe as you climb. A terrible blizzard blows up. You spot a building through the snow. Quick – get to shelter!

TURN TO PAGE 13 TO FIND OUT WHAT HAPPENS NEXT

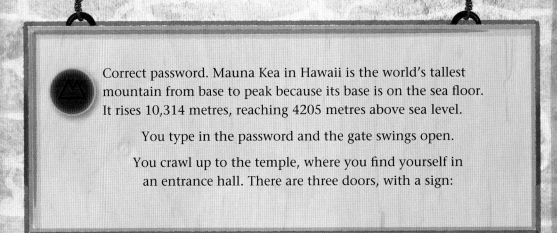

Correct password. Mauna Kea in Hawaii is the world's tallest mountain from base to peak because its base is on the sea floor. It rises 10,314 metres, reaching 4205 metres above sea level.

You type in the password and the gate swings open.

You crawl up to the temple, where you find yourself in an entrance hall. There are three doors, with a sign:

"TO FIND THE TRUTH, ENTER THE DOOR THAT ANSWERS THIS QUESTION:

Which mountain range contains the ten tallest mountains in the world?"

THE ALPS.
TURN TO PAGE 18

THE HIMALAYAS.
GO TO PAGE 21

THE ROCKIES.
HEAD TO PAGE 17

Wrong choice. You will definitely need sun cream. People burn easily in the wind and sunshine at high altitude, even in the cold.

TURN BACK TO PAGE 30 AND TRY AGAIN

 No, Ben Nevis isn't in France. It's the highest mountain in the British Isles, at 1344 metres.

TURN BACK TO PAGE 29 AND GUESS AGAIN

Correct answer. At an altitude of 3640 metres in the Andes Mountains, La Paz is the capital of Bolivia in South America. The woman opens the door.

Welcome to my station, I'm Marnie and I'm a meteorologist. Are you really a geographer? You can have a hot drink if you lend a hand with my research.

Can you help? What sort of station is run by a meteorologist?

A CABLE CAR STATION.
TURN TO PAGE 36

A METEOR RESEARCH STATION.
FLICK TO PAGE 41

A REINDEER-BREEDING STATION.
HEAD TO PAGE 38

A WEATHER STATION.
GO TO PAGE 42

That's right. About 10% of the world's population lives in the mountains, so mountain environments are very important to humans.

Yes, Sir Digby and his film crew spent the night here, then headed up the mountain. Look through my telescope at the different routes. People make money from all sorts of features in the mountains. But Sir Digby went in the one direction where there is no money to be made.

Which way did he go?

**NORTH PAST
THE CABLE CAR.**
TURN TO PAGE 41

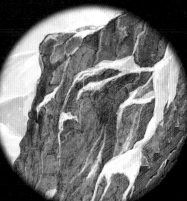

**WEST PAST
THE DAM.**
FLICK TO PAGE 10

**EAST PAST THE
HIGH CLIFFS.**
HEAD TO PAGE 20

**SOUTH PAST
THE LOGGERS.**
GO TO PAGE 43

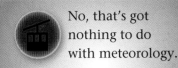

No, that's got nothing to do with meteorology.

TURN BACK TO PAGE 33 AND GUESS AGAIN

Wrong choice. Thick gloves are vital if you want to avoid frostbite in the freezing mountains.

TURN BACK TO PAGE 30 AND PICK AGAIN

That's right. The longest mountain range on the planet is the Mid Atlantic Ridge, which runs under the Atlantic Ocean for about 14,000 kilometres. That's 10 times the length of Great Britain.

We'll follow you up tomorrow. Oh, Digby also said he would build cairns from scree to mark his route.

You leave the mine and take the right-hand path. You stare up at the rocky mountainside.

What are cairns?

SNOWMEN.
TURN TO PAGE 18

PILES OF ROCKS.
GO TO PAGE 8

ARROWS MADE FROM TWIGS.
TURN TO PAGE 5

That's right. You step onto the glacier.

 Stop! You're not a glaciologist. Do you even know what a glacier really is?

Think quickly! What do you say?

A SLOWLY MOVING MASS OF ICE.

HEAD TO PAGE 41

A FROZEN RIVER.

GO TO PAGE 9

AN ICE DOME COVERING A MOUNTAIN SUMMIT.

TURN TO PAGE 16

No, K2 (on the border between Pakistan and China) is about 3000 metres from base to peak, even though its peak is 8611 metres above sea level.

TURN BACK TO PAGE 13 AND TRY AGAIN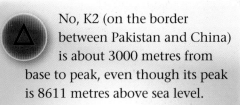

Nope. You're thinking of the Great Fire of London. People didn't start climbing mountains for sport until the 18th century.

GO BACK TO PAGE 10 AND TRY AGAIN

No! That's not right.

TURN BACK TO PAGE 20 AND TRY AGAIN

No, don't be fooled by Marnie's jumper.

GO BACK TO PAGE 33 AND THINK AGAIN

Correct choice. Malaria tablets stop you from catching a disease called malaria, which is spread by mosquitoes. These insects need warm temperatures (over 18°C) to survive, so the risk of catching malaria above 1500 metres is very low. The officer waves goodbye.

Before he vanished, Sir Digby was keeping an Internet blog, giving details of his movements. You use your phone to look at the first entry:

SIR DIGBY'S BLOG

3 November, 1300 hours

Left base camp at 0700 hours. Faced north then headed off at 45 degrees.

So which direction should you go?

SOUTHEAST.
GO TO
PAGE 5

NORTHEAST.
HEAD TO
PAGE 12

EAST.
TURN TO
PAGE 8

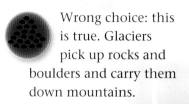 Wrong choice: this is true. Glaciers pick up rocks and boulders and carry them down mountains.

GO BACK TO PAGE 41 **AND HAVE ANOTHER GO**

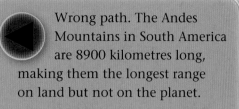 Wrong path. The Andes Mountains in South America are 8900 kilometres long, making them the longest range on land but not on the planet.

GO BACK TO PAGE 11 **AND TRY AGAIN**

 That's right. Mont Blanc means 'white mountain'.

I know! The combination could be the height of Mont Blanc.

It's worth a try! What combination do you enter?

8740 METRES.
GO TO PAGE 9
8740

7840 METRES.
HEAD TO PAGE 17
7840

4807 METRES.
TURN TO PAGE 43
4807

That's right. You open the box. There's a tangle of thick, white hair inside. Could it be yeti fur?

Ouch! A goat just head-butted you! You're surrounded by a herd.

Hello, I'm leading my goats to their winter pasture. I'll cook you supper if you take them while I round up my sheep.

You're getting hungry, so you decide to help – but the farmer's already disappeared. Where should you take the goats?

Is the winter pasture up or down the mountain?

UP.
TURN TO PAGE 42

DOWN.
HEAD TO PAGE 16

No, meteorology doesn't actually have anything to do with meteors.

GO BACK TO PAGE 33 AND TRY AGAIN

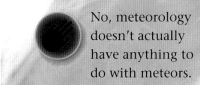

 Wrong direction. Cable cars help tourism, such as skiing, which is big business in the mountains.

TURN BACK TO PAGE 35 AND THINK AGAIN 1/10

 That's right. Over many years, mountain snow compacts (packs together), then the mass of ice moves slowly downhill.

Can I borrow a glove? Mine was torn off by the avalanche. My fingers will get frostbite.

Our boss says only qualified glaciologists are allowed our gear. If you can answer a glacier question, I'll assume you're qualified!

Which of these statements is false?

GLACIERS CAUSE EROSION.
GO TO PAGE 42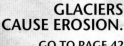

GLACIERS CARRY ROCKS.
FLICK TO PAGE 39

A GLACIER'S FRONT IS CALLED ITS CHIN.
TURN TO PAGE 28

No, it will be too cold higher up the mountain in winter.

**TURN BACK TO PAGE 40
AND THINK AGAIN** 1953

 Wrong choice: this is true. Glaciers cause erosion by crushing and scraping along the rock they move over.

**GO BACK TO PAGE 41
AND TRY AGAIN**

 Wrong answer. You're thinking of a gradient.

**TURN BACK TO PAGE 14
AND TRY AGAIN**

That's right. Meteorology is the study of the weather. Mountaintops are great places for researching the weather, atmosphere and clouds because they experience less pollution and are more exposed than other areas.

You help Marnie take some temperature readings until the blizzard dies down. Then you say goodbye to her and check Sir Digby's blog:

I'm at 4000 metres on a snowy slope with an easterly aspect. I can see huge footprints and I just heard a growl...

You must find the slope – but what's an easterly aspect?

**A SLOPE WITH
AN EASTERLY WIND.**
GO TO PAGE 8

**A SLOPE FACING
THE EAST.**
TURN TO PAGE 5

**A SLOPE FACING
THE WEST.**
HEAD TO PAGE 13

That's right. Mont Blanc is the highest mountain in the Alps of Europe – but much lower than Everest. You open the door.

There is a window at the end of the corridor. There's just time to grab the tray from Sir Digby's cell and hook your climbing rope to the window frame. You'll have to abseil down!

"*Stop!*" yells Bandit Bill behind you.

RUSH TO PAGE 24
TO MAKE YOUR ESCAPE – HURRY!

Wrong. At 8850 metres, Mount Everest is the highest summit in the world, but its two bases in Tibet and Nepal are 4200 to 5200 metres above sea level, so the height of the mountain itself is 3650 to 4650 metres.

TURN BACK TO PAGE 13
AND TRY AGAIN

Wrong direction. Logging can make lots of money.

GO BACK TO PAGE 35
AND TRY AGAIN

1/10

GLOSSARY

Abseil
To descend a rock face or vertical surface by using a rope.

Active volcano
A volcano that is currently erupting or that has erupted within historical time and is considered likely to erupt again in the future.

Altimeter
An instrument used for measuring altitude.

Altitude
Height above sea level.

Arête
A sharp, steep-sided ridge in an upland area, formed from the enlargement of corries.

Aspect
The direction in which a slope faces.

Avalanche
The rapid downwards movement of a mass of ice or snow. It is usually triggered by temperature rises or weakness in the snowpack (fallen snow that has been pressed down and hardened by its own weight).

Block mountain
A mountain or range of mountains formed by the uplift of blocks of rock along fault lines in the Earth's crust.

Blog
Website showing a series of entries that were written at different times.

Cairn

A pile of stones left as a marker.

Commercial farming

A type of farming in which crops and animals are produced to sell for a profit. In contrast, subsistence farming is when crops and animals are produced to feed just the farmer's family.

Corrie

Also known as a cirque or cwm, a corrie is a great bowl-shaped hollow at the head of a valley carved by a glacier. A corrie is formed when the weight of snow in a depression (sunken area) erodes the rock underneath over the course of hundreds of years.

Fold mountain

Fold mountain ranges are formed by the pushing together of two tectonic plates in the Earth's crust.

The pressure forces the edges of the plates upwards into a series of folds.

Glacial deposition

The laying down of rocks, debris and finer materials by glaciers.

Glacial erosion

The removal of rocky material by ice. Glacial erosion can shape the landscape, forming features such as U-shaped valleys, hanging valleys, arêtes and corries.

Glacier

A mass of ice formed by the build-up over many years of snow, compacting (pressing together) into a large body of ice that moves slowly down a slope or spreads outwards over a land surface.

Glaciologist

A scientist who studies glaciation by measuring and analysing the effects of ice and glaciers on the landscape.

Gradient
The steepness of a slope.

Hanging valley
A small valley carved by a glacier above a deeper, U-shaped valley eroded by a bigger glacier.

Intensive farming
A type of farming in which a large amount of food is produced from a small area of land. This is often achieved through the use of machinery, pesticides and fertilizers.

Logging
The cutting down of trees and transporting of the wood. Wood is used for a range of products, from paper to furniture.

Malaria
A disease caused by a parasite carried by a type of mosquito. Humans in many tropical areas can catch the disease from a single mosquito bite. Around 200 million people are infected each year and malaria is responsible for 500,000 deaths per year worldwide, 90% of them in Africa.

Meteor
A streak of light in the sky caused by a small chunk of rock or other matter from outer space entering the Earth's atmosphere. A meteor is often called a 'shooting star'.

Meteorologist
A scientist who studies the weather, atmosphere and climate.

Molten
Melted, usually by very great heat (as in the case of rocks inside the Earth).

Moraine
Debris deposited (laid down) by a glacier.

Plateau
A natural area of flattish highland, sometimes at great altitude.

Plate tectonics
The movement of large sections of the Earth's crust.

Ribbon lake
A long, narrow lake. Ribbon lakes are often found in troughs that have been eroded by a glacier.

Snowline
The lower edge of an area of permanent snow, often seen towards the summit of a mountain.

Terrace farming
A method of farming on steep slopes in which terraces, or steps, of flat ground are cut into the slopes.

Tourism
The industry catering for holidaymakers and travellers.

Volcanic mountain
A mountain formed when molten rock inside the Earth erupts and piles up at the surface.

Yeti
A hairy creature resembling a large ape. Some people think it lives high in the Himalayas, but its existence has never been proved. Also called the abominable snowman.

Taking it further

The Geography Quest books are designed to inspire children to develop and apply their geographical knowledge through compelling adventure stories. For each story, readers must solve a series of problems and challenges on their way to completing an exciting quest.

The books do not follow a page-by-page pattern. Instead, the reader jumps forwards and backwards through the book according to the answers given to the problems. If their answers are correct, the reader progresses to the next stage of the story; incorrect answers are fully explained before the reader is directed back to attempt the problem once again.

Additional help may be found in a glossary at the back of the book.

To support the development of your child's geographical knowledge, you can:

▲ Read the book with your child.

▲ Continue reading with your child until he or she has understood how to follow the 'Go to' instructions to the next puzzle or explanation, and is flipping through the book confidently.

▲ Encourage your child to read on alone. Prompt your child to tell you how the story develops and what problems they have solved.

▲ Point out the importance of mountain environments to our planet. Here are three questions: Why are there mountains? How do mountains affect many human activities? What difference would it make to life on the planet if the Earth were flat?

▲ Discuss what it would be like if you lived high in one of the greatest mountain ranges and how the habitat, environment and altitude might affect you.

▲ Take advantage of the many sources of geographical and geological information – libraries, museums and documentaries. The Internet is another valuable resource, and there is plenty of material specially aimed at children. Take care only to visit websites endorsed by respected educational authorities, such as museums and universities.

▲ Remember, we learn most when we're enjoying ourselves, so make geography fun!